OK Words

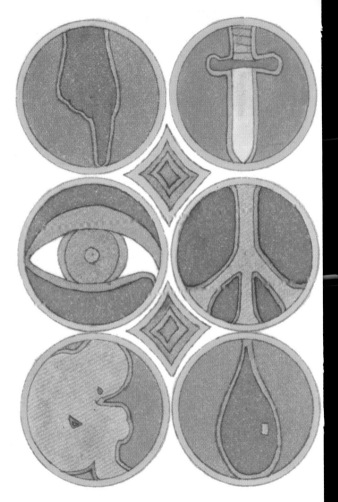

OK WORDS

From *I'M OK -- You're OK*

By Thomas A. Harris, M.D.

Illustrated by
John Overmyer

♕ Hallmark Editions

OK Words

I am a person.
You are a person.
Without you I am
not a person, for
only through you

is language made
possible and only
through language is
thought made
possible, and only
though thought is
humanness made possible.
You have made
me important.

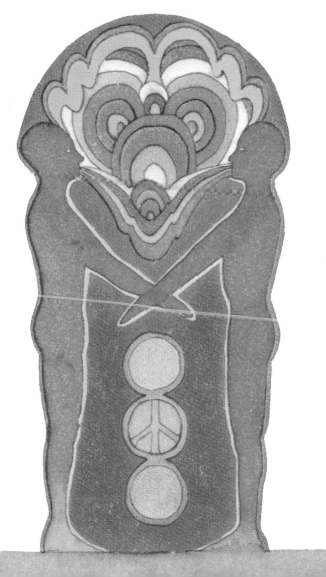

The individual is responsible for what happens in the future, no matter what has happened in the past. . . .

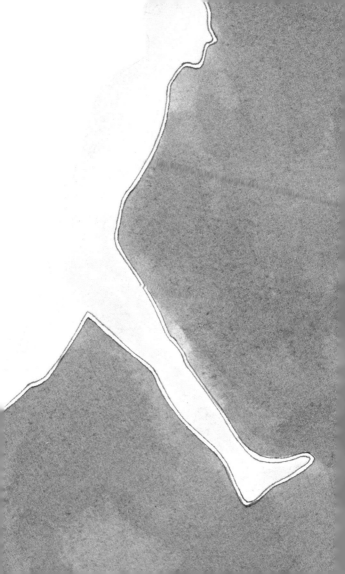

... and as long as people are bound by the past, they are not free to respond to the needs and aspirations of others in the present.

Intimacy is made possible
when beauty can be seen
apart from utility,
      when possessiveness
is made unnecessary by
  the reality of possession.

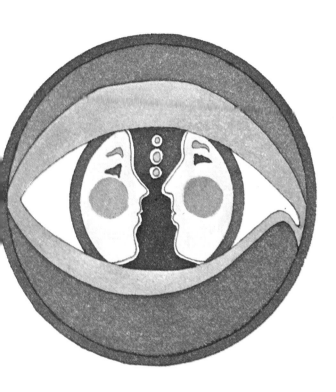

Giving and sharing
are spontaneous expressions
of joy.

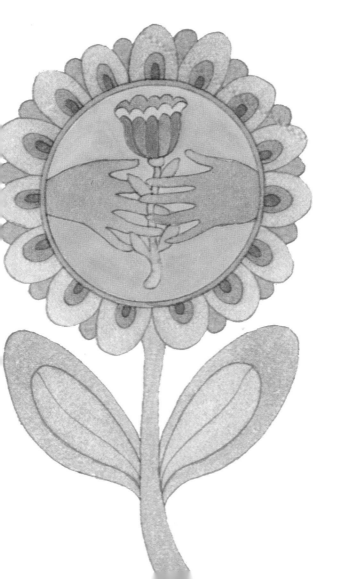

Slums and ghettos
are not going to disappear
in society unless slums
and ghettos disappear
from the hearts
of people.

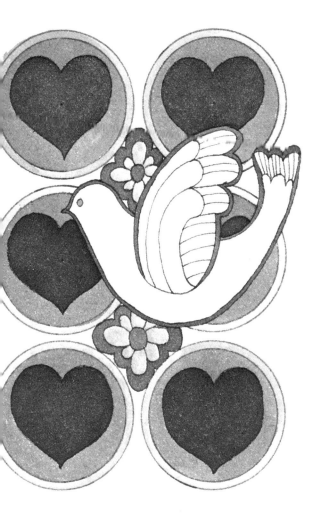

If we do not respond
to reason, our responses
will more and more be
dominated by fear.

It is the concentration
on communication
which will produce
something new
under the sun
rather than the ancient
recourse to
violence.

We can hate evil so much
that we forget to love
good.

And there is much that
is good.

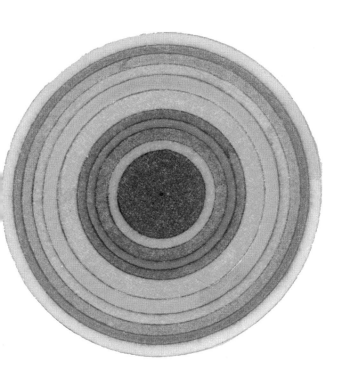

That man can aspire to
and achieve goodness
is evident
throughout all of history.

I am important
and
you are important.

If I devalue you,
I devalue myself.

Reality, for some people,
  is broader than it is
for others,

    because they have
        looked more,
          lived more,
         read more,
      experienced more,
      and thought more.

"I am like that"
does not help
anything.

"I can be different"
does.

The position
 I'M OK--YOU'RE OK
is a conscious and verbal
decision ~~based~~ on thought,
           faith,
     and the wager
       of action.

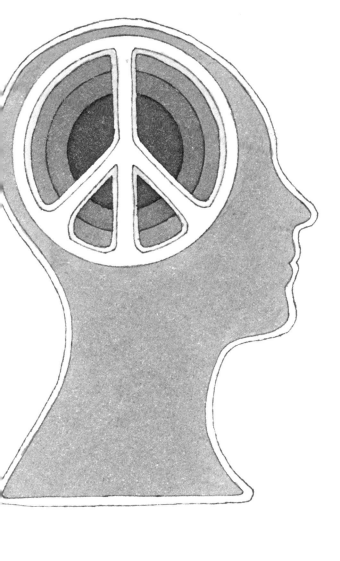

We may not understand
religious experience,
we may differ in its
explanation, but we
cannot, if we are
honest, deny the reports
of such experiences by
reputable men through
the centuries.

Persons are important in that they are all bound together in a universal relatedness which transcends their own personal experience.

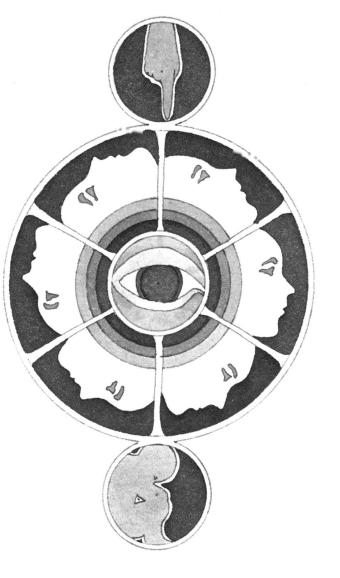

It takes only one generation
for a good thing to become
a bad thing, for an inference
to become dogma.
Dogma is the enemy
of truth and the enemy
of persons.
The ideas enshrined in
dogma may include
good and wise ideas,
but dogma is bad in
itself because it is
accepted as good
without examination.

People cannot and
        do not want to live
unrelated to other people.

We are responsible to
 and for one another,
and this responsibility is
the ultimate claim
 imposed on all
        men alike.

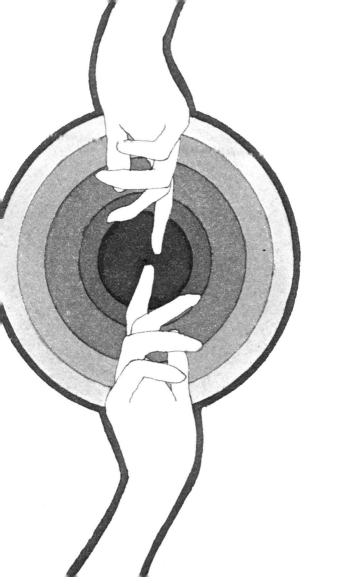

The people of the world
are not things to be manipulated,
but persons to know; not
heathen to be converted but
persons to be heard; not
enemies to be hated but
persons to be encountered;
not brothers to be kept
but brothers to be brothers.

If the relationship
between two people can be
made creative, fulfilling,
        and free of fear,

then this can work for
    two relationships,
or for relationships that
affect entire social groups,
        even nations....

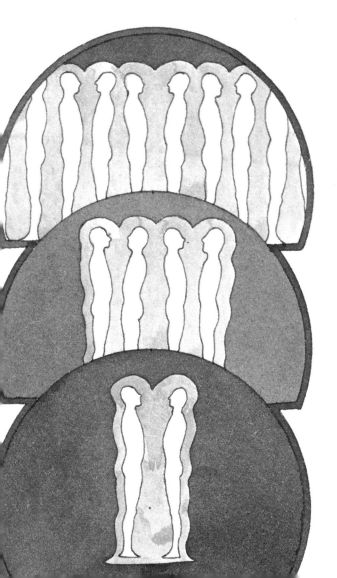

...The problems of
the world essentially are
the problems of individuals.

If individuals can
change, then the course
of the world can change.

This is a hope
worth sustaining.